Markers

FASTBACK® Sports

Markers

GEORGE WARREN

GLOBE FEARON
Pearson Learning Group

FASTBACK® SPORTS BOOKS

Claire	**Markers**
The Comeback	Redmond's Shot
Game Day	The Rookie
The Kid With the Left Hook	The Sure Thing
Marathon	Turk

Cover © Joel Rafkin/Times Record. All photography © Pearson Education, Inc. (PEI) unless specifically noted.

Copyright © 2004 by Pearson Education, Inc., publishing as Globe Fearon®, an imprint of Pearson Learning Group, 299 Jefferson Road, Parsippany, NJ 07054. All rights reserved. No part of this book may be reproduced or transmitted in any form or by any means, electronic or mechanical, including photocopying, recording, or by any information storage and retrieval system, without permission in writing from the publisher. For information regarding permission(s), write to Rights and Permissions Department.

Globe Fearon® and Fastback® are registered trademarks of Globe Fearon, Inc.

ISBN 0-13-024604-2
Printed in the United States of America
1 2 3 4 5 6 7 8 9 10   07 06 05 04 03

1-800-321-3106
www.pearsonlearning.com

"Don't be so restless," McCoy said. He bent over table Number Three in his pool room to pick a piece of dirt off the bright green cloth. "He'll be here, all right. He just wants to make you wait. He does it to all of them. Don't let him get to you."

In the dim light between the two tables, Shorty kept passing his cue stick from one hand to the other. He was all nerves. As McCoy watched, he reached up with the stick and shoved all the round scoring markers on the overhead wire to one side. Then he shoved them back into place again. "I can't sit still," he said. "It's the way I am."

McCoy looked at him closely. Shorty was lean and drawn. All the fat had been burned away by the fire inside him. "Relax," McCoy said. "You'll get your shot at him soon enough."

"My shot," Shorty said, pacing back and forth. "That's the right word for it. I'm gonna shoot him down. I'm gonna shoot out his lights."

McCoy watched him and didn't say anything for a while. Then he began to dig the balls out of the pockets and roll them over the green felt of the tabletop. He was in no hurry, and racked the balls with care. *Sure,* he thought. *You're gonna shoot him down.* A lot of people had said that, half an hour before facing the Parson in a big-money game. And one by one, the Parson had taken them all, for forty years now.

Still, if anyone could do it, Shorty might be the one. The little guy had come up very fast, and had beaten nearly all the top guns: Fresno Slim, Pockets Green, Fast Eddie Newman. Shorty had a good eye and a cool head, most of the time, and was a deadly hand with a bank shot. He'd hustled the best of them, from one end of California to the other, and had won a ton of money. It didn't matter that he never seemed to be able to keep any of it. On a good day he could lick just about anybody.

But the Parson?

McCoy watched as Shorty paced and cracked his knuckles. It made you jumpy just watching him. He was a bundle of nerves.

Well, that was what made you wonder about him in the end. The nerves. That, and the cold hate he felt for the Parson, and the way he envied the Parson's great cue stick, the one with the ivory inlays and the . . .

But now a ray of light from the front door broke through the gloom. McCoy looked up. "He's here, Shorty," he said. And the two of them watched the well-dressed old man walk slowly toward them, the whole length of the big empty room, past the bar and the jukebox.

McCoy took a quick look at Shorty. The little guy's eyes were not on the Parson's sour face, with its crown of white hair, or on his neat gray suit. They were on the smooth case he carried in his right hand, the one that held the Stick. Shorty's eyes seemed to shine in the dim light.

The Parson stopped and looked at both of them. "Hello," he said. "I understand somebody wants a game with me." He looked at them both, as if he didn't know which one. He knew. *He's a cool one,* McCoy thought.

"Somebody wants . . . ?" Shorty said. "Did you hear that?" He faced the Parson, hands on hips. "It's me. *I* want a game. I'm gonna take you for your shirt, old man."

"McCoy," The Parson said, "next time don't call me for this penny-ante low ball stuff. It isn't worth taking my stick out of its case." He turned as if to go. He did not look at Shorty.

"Hey," Shorty said. "Look at me, you . . ."

The Parson *did* look at him just then, and his face was icy. "Do you think I don't know you?" he said. "Peanuts games. Playing for carfare. Nickels and dimes. You never put up a decent stake in your life. And that's why you don't amount to anything now, and never will."

"Hey, you can't say . . ."

"What are you saying?" the Parson said, his tone hard. "That we should play one-pocket for $100 a shot? Or do you expect me to give credit? To take your marker?

You, who never paid a back bill in your life?"

"You! You got a lot of room to talk!"

The Parson wasn't listening to him now, though. He had turned to McCoy, the cue-stick case under his arm, and he was getting ready to go. "Call me again when there's some real action, will you, McCoy? I'll see you around."

McCoy wasn't sure why he did it. Maybe he wanted to see them play. Maybe he just wanted to see that Stick in action again, that lovely inlaid cue. But somehow he found himself saying, "Hey, give him a break, Parson. Hear him out. I think he's on the level."

The Parson stopped and stared. Then he looked at Shorty. "How much have you got?" he said, his voice all business.

Shorty gulped. "I . . . I got $1200. But . . ."

The Parson let out a snort. "$1200. Well, all right. For $1200, then. Nine-ball, best three games out of five."

"B-but my game's one-pocket . . ."

"I know it is. Take it or leave it."

Shorty blinked—and went for it. The way things were, what other choice did he have? McCoy racked the balls on table Number Two, the best one in the house. Shorty won the toss for the break.

You could see it was a pro's game. Shorty was hot and took the first game with ease, playing position like a grand master. He ran the last six balls and sank the nine on a perfect bank shot. He was all business—except when the Parson was shooting. Then his eyes, burning with greed, went over to the Parson's beautiful cue stick with its long polished shaft and the inlaid handle. That was the stick that Ralph Greenleaf had given to him. The Parson had won the world title with it back in the forties.

Shorty broke again, and sank two balls on the break. Then he ran out the table, shooting like a champ himself, finally dropping the nine in the side with as soft a kiss shot as McCoy had ever seen. And as he called for the rack, his eyes went once more to the cue in the old man's hand. "You're down two," he said.

But the Parson just stood there, looking

him up and down coldly. You could tell he didn't think much of Shorty. "You're pretty sure of yourself," he said. "It's likely because the stakes are so low." He snorted again. "What am I doing, wasting my time like this? Look, McCoy . . ."

"Hey," Shorty said. "In a couple minutes I'll have $2400. Then, I'll play you double or nothing, and . . ."

"Peanuts," the old man said. "Now, if we could start with . . . oh, say, ten thousand . . ." But he waved the thought away with a scowl. "Where would you get ten thousand from, anyhow? No, it's a waste of time." He started to walk away.

"Hey!" Shorty said. "Wait! Look, I can't raise it right now. But I'm hot today. If I could play for markers . . ."

The Parson turned and stared at him

coldly. "Your *marker*?" he said. "For ten grand? Against my cash?"

Shorty's eyes blinked. He wiped his sweaty palms. "Against your cash," he said, hoarsely. "Five grand of your cash—and your cue stick."

Now it was out. Shorty looked nervously at McCoy and the Parson, one after the other, licking his lips. They both knew what was on his mind now. And all three of them knew that it wasn't just a money match any more. It was a grudge match. Shorty wanted the old man's hide now, bad. He wanted not only to beat him, but to put him out of business. And the one way to do that was to take that magic Stick away from him.

The Parson sighed—and almost smiled. "All right," he said. "Why didn't you talk stakes like that in the first place?" He nodded to McCoy. "You're our witness, McCoy. Now could you rack 'em up, please?"

There were a few people in the table-side chairs now. They had just drifted in and gotten the picture that something special was going on here. As they watched, Shorty ran three balls after the break—and then the tide turned. The Parson, hidden behind the six ball, sank the four on a perfect bank shot and went on to run the table. That shiny Stick of his flashed in the table light and struck again and again, like a tiger. And after

McCoy racked the balls again, the Parson sank the nine-ball on the break. It was two games to two, now. On this fifth game, they'd be playing for more money than Shorty had ever had at one time in his whole life.

The Parson paused before the break, and looked at Shorty with eyes that had become almost gentle. Then he looked down at the Stick in his hand. "You're right," he said. "It *is* quite a prize, one worth going into the hole for. Anyone who gets his hands on it will win a lot of games with it. And a lot of dough. But you're not going to get it easily. I'm going to make you earn it."

Then he smiled, and it was a strange smile indeed, cold and warm at the same time. And he leaned forward, took two practice strokes, and broke, sinking the three-ball in the side.

Now, the people out in the darkness beyond the circle of light stopped whispering. They seemed to be holding their breaths as the Parson bent over the table. When the next ball fell, they looked, not at the Parson, but at Shorty. The little guy's dark eyes were shiny, and his face was drawn.

The Parson missed one now, but he left Shorty with no shot at all. Shorty just managed to touch his object ball and sent the cue ball to the far end of the table. The Parson now had an almost impossible shot. He shot—and missed the object ball by an inch. A foul! "Cue ball in hand to Shorty," McCoy said calmly, handing Shorty the ball.

Shorty's face had a winner's smile. He held the white cue ball—and looked once more at the Stick in the Parson's hand. He put the ball down in just the right place and sighted along his own cue. He sank the six, seven, and eight, and wound up with a long cut shot on the nine, at the far end of the table. "Corner pocket," he said. Then he bent over the table and stroked the ball.

The nine ball, barely touched at all, rode slowly along the rail toward the pocket—and hung, and did not fall.

The Parson could have made the shot Shorty had left him with one arm tied behind his back. He calmly sank the nine ball. Game and match to the Parson!

Shorty let out a long deep breath, and closed his eyes. When he opened them the

Parson was taking apart the beautiful cue stick carefully. Shorty, stunned, watched the old man pack it away inside its case.

The Parson said, matter-of-factly, "You owe me $1200 right now. I'll take it with me. That leaves a balance of $8800. I'll expect it within a reasonable amount of time. You can leave it with McCoy here." He picked up the cue-stick case and tucked it under one arm. He looked sharp and well-dressed and alert. "What do you want to bet he doesn't pay up, McCoy," he said. "Once a small-timer, always a small-timer."

Suddenly, McCoy felt a flash of anger. "Lay off, Parson," he said. "He'll pay up." He looked at Shorty's drawn face and glazed eyes, and wondered.

The Parson chuckled, not pleasantly.

"Will he?" he said. "I wouldn't bet the rent money on it if I were you. He's a nobody. He'll never amount to anything." His eyes looked right through Shorty and didn't see him any more. "Could you collect the $1200 for me, McCoy? I'm going to the bathroom." He put the case down on the table and went back into the dark part of the room.

Both men followed him with their eyes all the way to the bathroom door. There was an awkward silence as the crowd began to slip away, one by one. Then Shorty tossed a roll of bills onto the green cloth and started taking his own stick apart to stow it away. "I'll . . . I'll show him," Shorty said through clenched teeth, his voice shaking. "I'll have the dough for you in three months, McCoy. Three months. Every nickel of it." But as he turned to walk slowly all the way to the front door, he looked shorter and more like a small-timer than ever.

McCoy was alone when the Parson came out patting his hands dry with his handkerchief. "Don't tell me, McCoy," he said. "I know what you're going to say. You're going to tell me I was too hard on him."

"It's not my business," McCoy said. His voice was tight and cold. "You're wrong, though. He'll be back. He'll pay up."

"Oh, I know that," the Parson said. He picked up the roll of bills and put it in his pocket. "He hates my guts now. Nothing in the world can stop him now. He'll do whatever it takes to get the dough together three months from now. And he'll come back not with ten thousand in his pocket. He'll have fifteen, twenty. He'll want to wave it under my nose and show me." His voice could barely be heard, though, when he added, "It'll be a pity to disappoint him."

McCoy, busy racking the balls, almost missed it. But then, he stopped what he was doing and looked at the Parson. The old man's face looked tired and sad. "Disappoint him?" McCoy said. "I don't get it."

The Parson looked at him, blankly. "McCoy, you're a little thick today. I haven't *got* three months. I won't be around when he gets back." McCoy stared with an open mouth. "I'll let you in on another little secret, too. I haven't got ten grand on me. I haven't even got five."

"You've been bluffing?" McCoy said. "A high roller like you?"

"I used to have it," the Parson said. "But it's been going out the door, going to the doctors and the clinic, faster than my Stick here can bring it back in again. And now . . . well, I talked to the doctor yesterday. He gives me maybe six weeks."

"Well, I'll be . . ." McCoy's voice was suddenly gentle.

"Yeah. That's what I said. And that's

not a lot of time to start putting your things in order, is it? Paying off old markers. Cleaning up after yourself. Making up for things you did to people."

"Aw, come on, Parson," McCoy said, his voice hoarse. "You never did anything to anybody. You've been straight with people, most of the time."

"What do you know about it?" the Parson said. "You just stand there and rack the balls and collect the table fees. You don't even know what color car I drive." He sighed. "Well, it's too late to get anybody to forgive me. It always is. But at least maybe I can pay off my markers, and maybe look myself in the eye again before I go."

"I . . . I don't get this," McCoy said. "You say all this, right after pulling a sucker trick like that on the kid? After conning him that way? I don't understand you, Parson. I don't understand you at all."

"He's not a bad kid, is he? And he's a sure thing. I didn't have a better eye than that myself, when I was his age. No, and neither did Wimpy Lassiter or Mosconi. I know. I played those guys. He's as good as the best of them. Tough, cool, talented." He held up the Stick in its case. "He *could* be more confident, maybe. You know, he thinks that having this thing would give it to him." He chuckled. "Why, it's only a stick. It isn't even the same one Greenleaf gave me, the one I used in the title match. Somebody stole that one years ago, and I had another one made. I just didn't tell anybody. It makes a better story this way."

"I think I'm beginning to understand you," McCoy said in a strange voice. "I think I'm catching on."

"What the kid really needs is focus. Something to get—well, everything in his whole system all zeroed in on winning, so that he doesn't think of anything else. So that he'll just come up to a problem, look it over, and do whatever it takes to solve it. The guy who wins is always the guy who'll do whatever it takes. Whatever."

McCoy started to speak, but something caught in his throat and he had to try again. "Whatever it takes," he said. "Including beating somebody so bad that he'll hate you enough to get his act together at last. And then he'll get up a decent stake for a change, and make something of himself."

"McCoy," the Parson said, "you're not as dumb as I thought." He coughed into his hand and when he looked back at McCoy his face seemed more tired than ever.

"Look," he said. "This kid—there's more to him than there was to me. Me, I could shoot pool. That was it. I was a lousy husband. I was a lousy father. After a while, I quit faking it and took off. It was what I needed. It wasn't what *he* needed just then, or his mother either."

"Shorty?" McCoy said. "*Shorty's your kid?*" But he knew the answer before he asked.

The Parson ignored the question. "She

never forgave me. Look, who can blame her? And the kid never did either. That's okay. But she went to her grave holding a marker of mine. I can't do anything about hers, but the kid holds one too. And . . ."

"All right, all right," McCoy said. His back was turned. He wiped his nose. "So when he comes in with the dough, I tell him to give it to charity?"

"You tell him to take it over to Vegas and stick it up Flagstaff Whitey's nose, or Paddy Gleason's. If he can't take those guys for six figures with a stake like that, I'm a boy scout."

McCoy turned to look at him now. "Flagstaff Whitey?" he said. "You really think he's ready for him?"

The Parson stuck the cue case under his arm and straightened his tie. "Why not?"

he said. "He was ready for *me*, wasn't he?" He brushed back the white hair at his temples with his palms. "Well, see you around, McCoy. And look, when you see the kid tell him . . ." But he stopped dead, letting the words trail off. And for a moment his eyes were focused on something far away. "Well, never mind. Give him this." He handed over the Stick in its neat little case, and winked at McCoy. "Tell him he'll need a special stick like this, going up against those guys. A champion's stick. One that used to belong to Ralph Greenleaf."

And then he turned and walked away, his back as straight as ever. "Markers," he said, as he went out the door.